when the WHALE
came to my town

by JIM YOUNG

Photographs by
DAN BERNSTEIN

SCHOLASTIC BOOK SERVICES
NEW YORK • TORONTO • LONDON • AUCKLAND • SYDNEY • TOKYO

Text copyright © 1974 by Jim Young. Photographs copyright © 1974 by Dan Bernstein. This edition is published by Scholastic Book Services, a division of Scholastic Magazines, Inc., by arrangement with Alfred A. Knopf, Inc.

12 11 10 9 8 7 6 5 4 3 2 1   4   6 7 8 9/7 0 1/8
07

Printed in the U.S.A.

There's one time I'll never forget. Never, as long as I live. That's when the whale came to our town.

I live in Provincetown at the very tip of Cape Cod, where the Pilgrims first landed. Behind my house is the beach and beyond that is the Atlantic Ocean. Every day I walk along the beach. Even on school days because that's the way I go to school. On the way home when I pass the wharf I look to see if my father's boat is in.

My father goes out early every morning to fish for perch and mackerel, flounder and tuna. When I grow up I want to be a fisherman like my father. My grandfather was a fisherman too. He fished for lobster in the summer and codfish in the winter. My great-grandfather hunted whales.

I never want to hunt for whales.

A hundred years ago every man in my town hunted for whales. They would go off in big ships with sails and stay at sea sometimes for as long as three years. That's what my great-grandfather did.

My grandfather's boat had sails too. But my father's boat is a dragger. No sails.

From my father's boat I've seen whales swimming just outside our harbor. They let us come so close that I thought they wanted to make friends.

Whales are big and strong, and smart too. They know things no man knows. They breathe air but can live in the deepest water. Whales swim faster and live longer than almost anything in the sea.

The whale is like a big elephant, like the moon and the sun.

I never want to hunt for whales.

That day it was cold and windy, the middle of winter. I was on my way to school and alone on the beach. The sky was full of dark clouds. The tide was going out.

I saw a big gray thing. It was half on the sand and half in the water. A dead thing bigger than a bus.

I looked at it and I knew what it was.

It was the biggest thing I had ever seen on our beach. Maybe it was the biggest thing ever to come to our beach. The biggest thing alive or dead. Ever.

I was alone with it. And afraid.

No one was on the beach but me and it. Not even a gull. There are always lots of gulls on the beach at low tide and most mornings beach dogs are there too. But this morning there was just me and it. And it was dead and big. I knew what it was and I guess I was afraid.

I walked closer. There were no crabs on it. Crabs always crawl over dead things from the sea. And it was right side up. Dead fish are usually upside down when they wash onto the beach. It was right side up and it gave a windy sound. It was a whale. And it was alive. I could hear it breathe and see an eye move. Its skin was still wet and it was sparkling like silver.

Whales have skin. They don't have scales and they don't have fins like fish because they aren't fish. And they have big flukes for a tail.

The whale's flukes moved slowly in the water and I got my shoes wet walking around him. The tide was going out and pretty soon the whale was all the way out of the water. He was half buried in the sand where he lay.

It was a long time before it would be high tide again and the whale could swim away. He was stranded on the sand. Now I could walk around him without getting my feet wet.

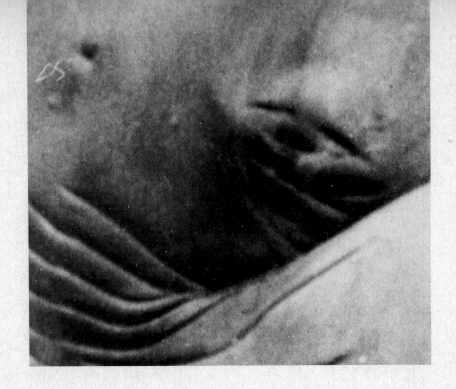

He had tiny eyes. Black eyes. Every once in a while his eye would blink. I could see only one eye at a time because the other was all the way around on the other side of his head.

He had a big mouth, and a big head too. The biggest head of any animal I can think of. Bigger than a buffalo. Bigger than an elephant.

Steam was coming from a hole on top of his head. A whale breathes through its spout and spouts water through its spout. But this whale was spouting steam.

I listened to his breathing sound. Why was he here? Was he lost? Did he chase something into shallow water? Was he old? Was he a she? And going to have a baby whale on the beach? I know that sea turtles come out of the sea to lay their eggs in the sand. But whales don't lay eggs.

I've heard people in our town say that when whales want to die they swim to shore sometimes.

Was this whale dying?

I didn't go to school that day. I stayed with the whale. All day.

But first I went home to tell about the whale. And then I told everybody on the street.

No one in my house believed me when I said there was a live whale on the beach. Once I told my mother I saw a bear in the sand dunes so I guess that's why she didn't believe in live whales on our beach.

I wish I never told the people in my town about the whale I found.

The old men were the first to come down to the beach to see the whale. Their dogs came too. The dogs ran around the whale and barked. The old men stood way back and talked.

Old men know something about everything. They can remember the days when our town was still a whaling town. They are too old to fish now so they talk about fishing. They love to talk almost as much as they love their dogs.

My father says the three things our town loves the most are its old men, its children and its dogs.

The dogs barked. The old men talked.

Whales of the olden times — that's what they talked about. About the whale in the Bible and how Jonah became a good man when he was inside that whale's stomach. And how the Eskimos pray to whales. They talked about whales from the South Seas that gave whale oil to be burned in lamps. That was before electricity was discovered, and before I was born. Before my father was born too. But not before this whale was born.

The whale looked very old. He had lots of wrinkles all over. More wrinkles than the old men. He must have been a thousand years old.

All day long people kept coming and going.

In the afternoon the kids came and I knew school was out. Some of the boys poked their fingers in the whale's side and then yelled and jumped back. They were afraid. The old men said they better watch out or the whale would swallow 'em up.

Then the gulls came – hundreds of them – and flew over the whale. Where had they been all morning? Had they been afraid too? They made loud cries and more noise than all the people and all the dogs put together.

Even with my fingers in my ears I could still hear the cry of the gulls. *Wait! Wait! Wait!* It sounded like that, it really did.

All day long people kept coming and going. I wished I had never told anyone about the whale. I wished the whale had gone away before all the town people had come. I wished the beach didn't have a town at all.

My father came back from fishing to see the whale. I was glad he was there. He looked at it and I could tell he was sad.

The whale didn't sparkle like silver anymore. He was still completely out of the water and his skin was dry.

The dogs were fighting. The kids were fighting.

The people were arguing. The gulls were crying.
And light was going from the sky.

Everyone went home.

Wait! Wait! Wait! cried the gulls.

I didn't care about dinner if I had to leave the
whale. So my father brought me a sandwich and I
stayed until night. I never ate my sandwich. I guess
the crabs got it. Crabs will eat anything any time.

The tide was coming in and I was alone with the
whale again. I listened to him breathe. His flukes
made a soft slapping sound in the water. I looked at
his black eye and walked around to the other side
to see his other eye. I looked at his eye for a long
time and his eye looked at me. Then he blinked.
And I wasn't afraid anymore.

When my father came to get me it was high tide
and the whale was as black as the water and the
night.

And that was the first day that the whale came to
our town.

That night I had a big dream. Not about me. About whales. Lots of whales. Baby whales, children whales, mother whales and father whales. There was a king whale too. I couldn't see him very well because he lived inside a white fog. The fog moved and from it came little clouds of gray fog that turned into more whales. Herds of whales.

Was this whale heaven?

I liked my dream. It was beautiful.

The next morning I was up very early to see if my whale was still there. He must have moved with the tide during the night and was floating near the old tumble-down wharf. In the olden times whaling ships used to tie up at that wharf, but now only seagulls go there.

That's where the whale was. Floating in the surf. The tide was going out so I knew that soon he would be on the sand again.

The town people came back to see the whale. They said my whale was dying.

I sat on the beach and watched the sun rise in the sky and the tide go way out. Pretty soon there was no water around the whale. I could hear him breathe. His skin looked like silver, and white steam came from his spout. He was still alive.

I watched him and thought about him for a long time. Did he know where he was? Did he know what was happening?

They said my whale was dying. They said he was going to die on the beach and he would make a great big stink when he was dead. A stink worse than the town dump, they said, and the smell would poison the air. They said it would take a month of Sundays for the crabs and gulls to do away with the whale so the town had better do something about it.

They talked and talked. I tried to shut my ears to their words but I could still hear the dogs barking and the gulls crying.

Wait! Wait! Wait!

Was the whale dying? Maybe he knew he was dying and didn't care about the people saying he would make a big stink. Maybe he was thinking about whale heaven like in my dream . . . maybe he was. But it was very hard for me to think about my whale dying

The dogs didn't bark so much on the second day. They chased the gulls.

Wait! Wait! Wait! cried the gulls all that day.

It was warm for winter and I think the whale was very hot. His skin wasn't silver now. It looked like lead. As the day got warmer his breath came faster. He didn't do anything but breathe and steam. So most of the people went home for lunch.

In the afternoon a man from the Animal Rescue League came with a pump and a hose and sprinkled the whale. He said that whales have to be wet and cool to live.

There was hot sun all day long. So the man stayed and sprinkled the whale to keep him cool. His skin sparkled like silver again.

He sprinkled the whale until the tide came in. He sprinkled it until the Coast Guard boat came in with the tide. The sailors were waiting for the whale to float. They wanted to tow him out into the harbor so they tied a rope around his flukes.

On the beach the people waited and watched. They watched the Coast Guard tow the whale out into the black harbor, backwards. They towed him by his flukes. Backwards is no way for a whale to go out to sea.

Wait! called the gulls. And the dogs began to bark again.

Then there was a huge splash and I knew what had made it. The Coast Guard boat wasn't moving so I knew the rope had broken. The whale was swimming to shore again. He was swimming very fast, so fast he came right up onto the beach.

The whale lay on the beach, steaming and breathing. Clouds darkened the sky and a wind blew from the east.

That was the first time they towed my whale out into the harbor.

A man came who knew a lot about whales. He wore a stethoscope around his neck so he could listen to the whale's heart. He said they didn't often get to listen to a live whale's heart. He didn't come to make the whale well. He said he came to learn from the whale.

He listened to the whale's heart for quite a while. He said whales have very big hearts and that my whale was sick but his heart was still good. He didn't say what had made him sick.

He took the whale's temperature and said the whale was too hot, much too hot. So the man from the Animal Rescue League sprinkled the whale again.

Then the Coast Guard boat came back with another rope – a bigger one. The sailors tied it around the whale's flukes.

The whale doctor wanted the Coast Guard to wait. He wanted to hear the whale's heart some more and take his temperature again. He said they could learn a lot by studying the sick whale. But the Coast Guard wouldn't wait.

The sky was getting darker and the wind blew harder. Night was coming too. Night comes early in the winter when dark clouds are over the harbor.

Wait! Wait! Wait! cried the gulls.

They towed the whale back out into the black harbor. It was so dark now you couldn't see too well. And windy too. But this time the Coast Guard boat didn't come back and my whale didn't come back either.

It began to rain and then the big storm came. My father took me home and I sat in front of the fireplace to get warm and dry.

That night I had another whale dream. A whale took me for a ride around the world. Clear around the whole world. We swam through fire. We swam through ice. We swam around rocks and under ships and dived under floating islands.

We swam into the harbor of my own town. There was a big stink in the harbor so we swam away. We were looking for whale heaven.

This was the second whale dream I ever had.

When I woke up the storm was over. My mother made me eat breakfast before I went to see about my whale. All the time I was eating I was thinking about him and wondering if he was back on the beach now that the storm had passed.

I guess my whale was the first one on the beach that day. And by the time I got there the Coast Guard boat was there too. The doctor was there. The old men were there. The dogs were there. And the gulls were crying.

Wait! Wait! Wait!

The whale was tired and was lying on his side. This was his third day on our beach.

More doctors came in jeeps to see the whale and listen to his heart. The sailors tied another big rope around his flukes and then waited . . . for the tide, I guess. The old men watched and talked about the storm.

The doctors spent lots of time around the whale that day. They put wires all over his body. I don't know why. They knew a lot about whales and said they were finding out more. But none of them knew why the whale swam back to shore after the storm. I know that when I get tired swimming I swim to shore.

Wait! cried the gulls.

Three times that day the Coast Guard towed the whale out into the harbor. Once he broke another rope and twice the Coast Guard let him loose from way out and he swam back anyway. So three more times the whale swam back to shore.

Wait ... *Wait* ... *Wait* ... cried the gulls all day long.

Late in the afternoon the doctors went home in their jeeps. The old men stayed a while and talked. Then they went home too. The dogs followed them. The sailors left in the Coast Guard boat, and the tide went out.

The sun was setting and everyone had gone home but the gulls and me.

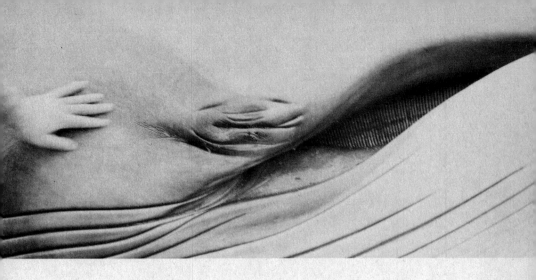

The whale was lying on the sand again. He didn't want to swim in the sea anymore. He was on the beach and he was tired.

I was alone with him. I wanted to say goodbye. I had never touched my whale.

The gulls were circling high above me and the whale.

His skin was shining like red-gold in the late afternoon sun. I put my hand on his gold skin and patted him once. I could feel his big body shake under my hand. I patted him goodbye.

Why? said the gulls.

Was my whale a pilgrim of the sea who came to shore?

He opened his mouth. It was like a big cave. Bigger than a cave. Three times he opened his mouth and I was afraid when I saw the cave. The gulls were afraid and flew away.

The whale died then. He died on the beach behind my house.

That was the third day and the last day the whale came to my town.